READABOUT

Measurement

This edition 2003

Franklin Watts
96 Leonard Street
London EC2A 4XD

Franklin Watts Australia
45-51 Huntley Street
Alexandria
NSW 2015

Editor: Ambreen Husain
Design: K and Co

Additional Photographs:
ZEFA pp. 12 and 13

A CIP catalogue record for this book is available from the British Library.

ISBN 0 7496 5273 X

Printed in Hong Kong

READABOUT

Measurement

Text: Henry Pluckrose
Photography: Chris Fairclough

W
FRANKLIN WATTS
LONDON • SYDNEY

There are some things you need to know… like the size of shoe you wear.

You can have your feet measured.
The measure gives the length and width of each foot.

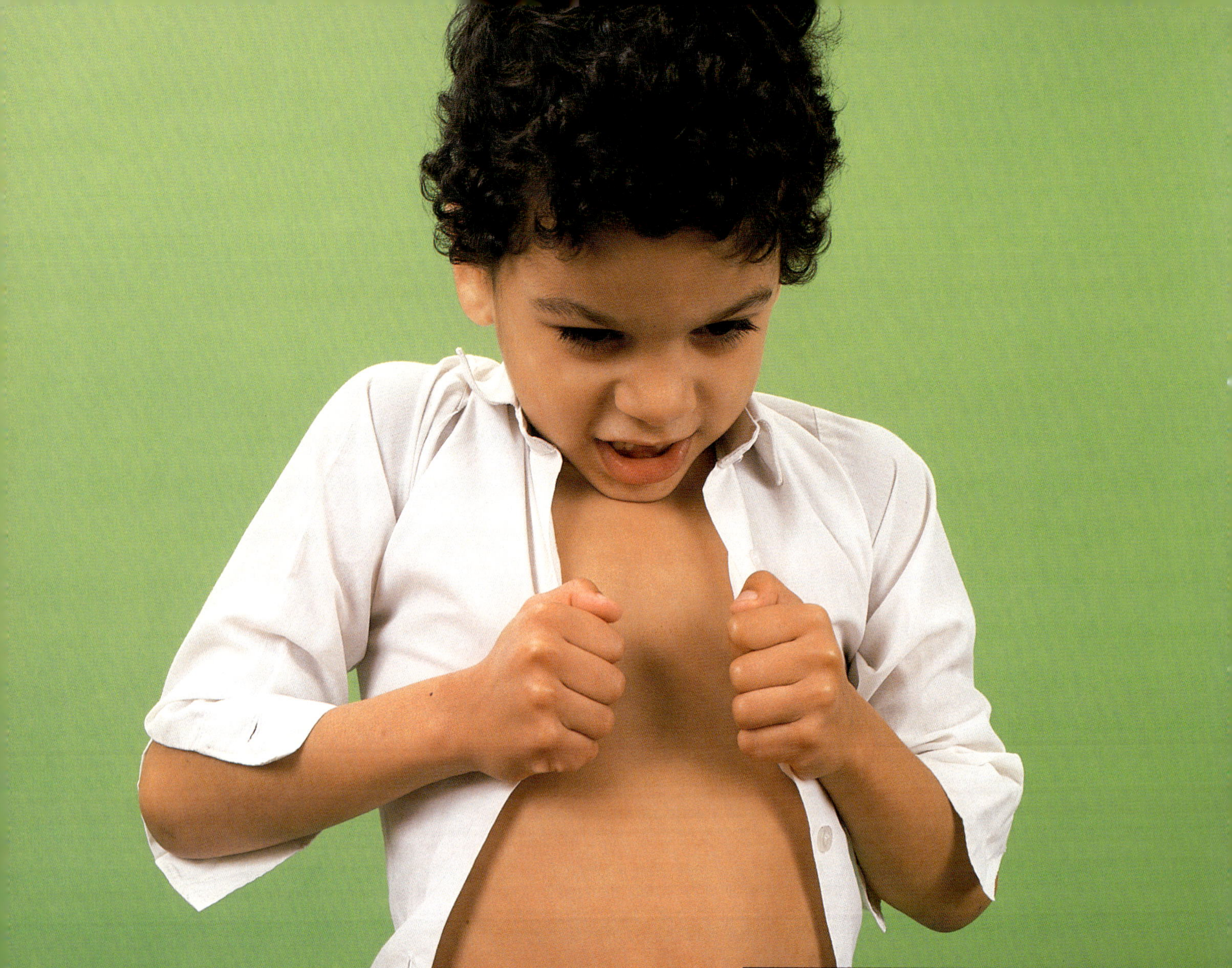

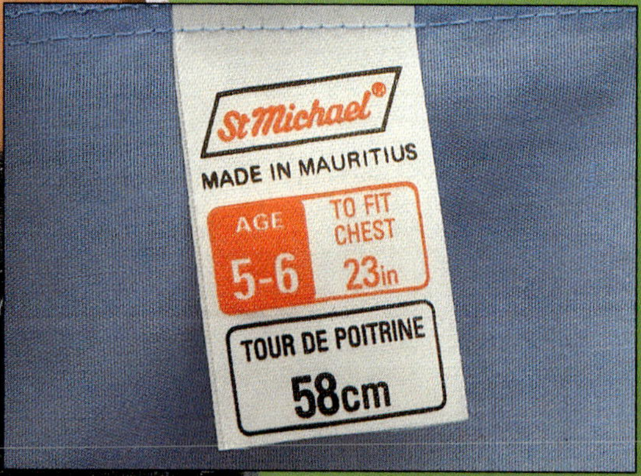

When you buy clothes
they should fit you.
The numbers on the labels
give the sizes.

Do you know
what size you are?

We use numbers to measure.
We need something else too.
How long is the toy car?
It is 8 centimetres long.
The centimetre is
a measure of length.

You can also measure your height in centimetres. How tall are you?

Centimetres are useful for measuring small lengths. It would be difficult to measure this tennis court in centimetres.

You could use a metre stick,
a tape
or a click wheel.
How many centimetres
make one metre?

The kilometre is 1,000 metres. It is used in many countries to measure long distances.

In some countries, long distances are measured in miles.

When you are ill
your temperature is taken.
A thermometer is used
to find out
whether you are hot
and feverish.

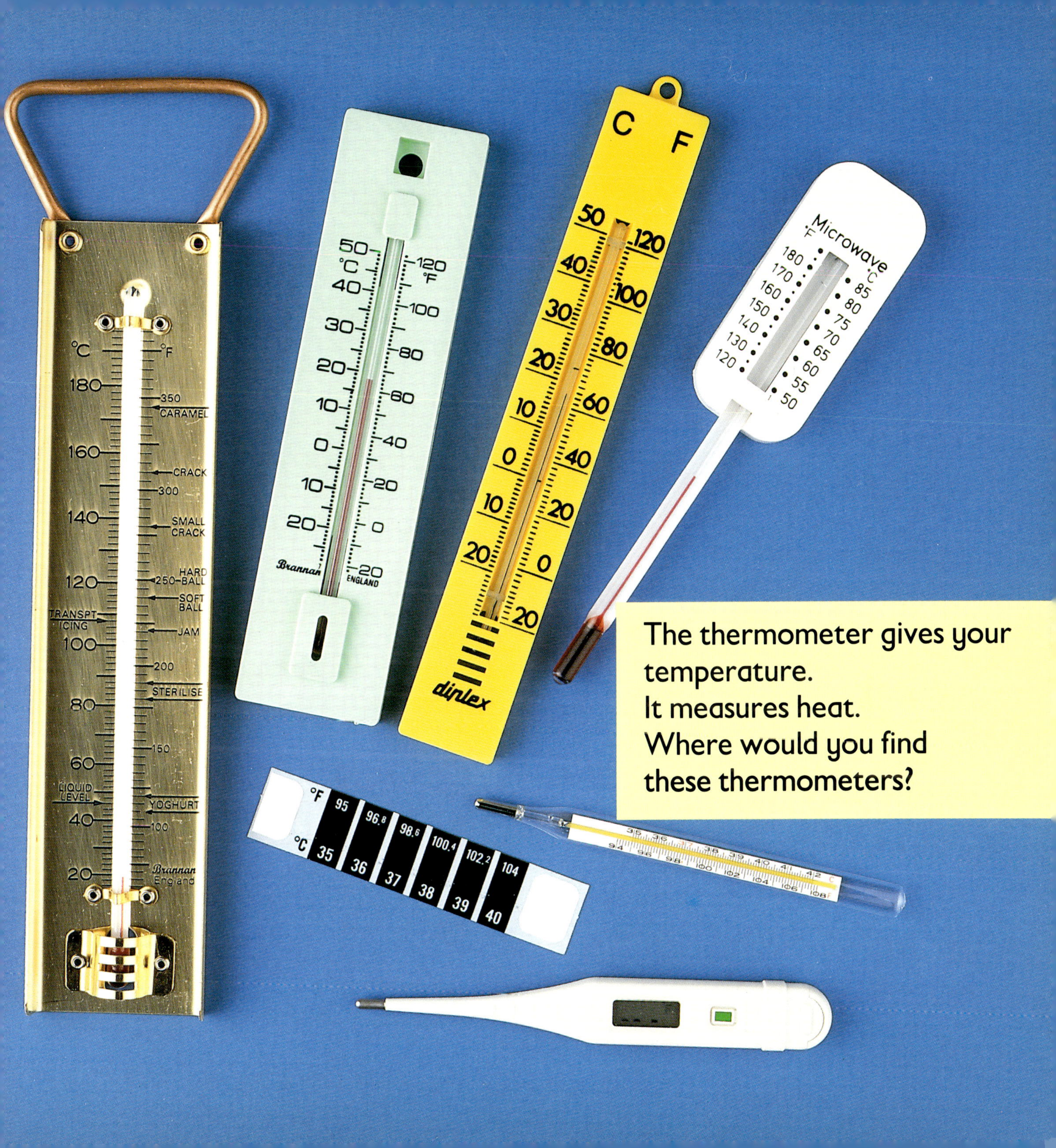

The thermometer gives your temperature.
It measures heat.
Where would you find these thermometers?

We need to be able to measure in other ways.
You can not take a temperature with a ruler...

or buy potatoes by the metre.

We need to be able to measure how heavy things are.
This scale weighs things which are very light.

Scales like these are used for weighing food. The kilogram weight balances the kilogram of apples. The kilo is a measure of weight.

Here are some more scales
and balances.
What kind of things could you
weigh on them?

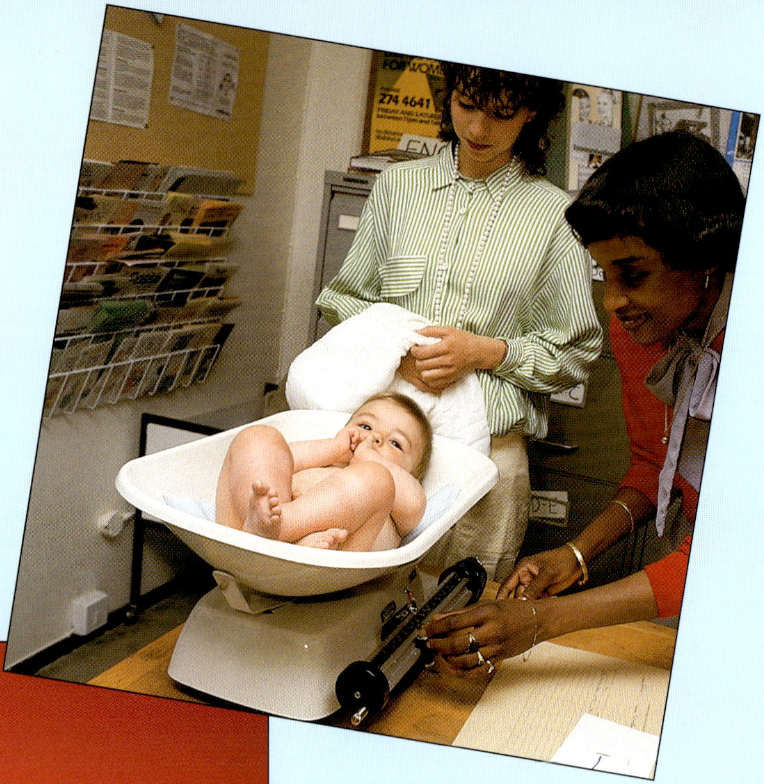

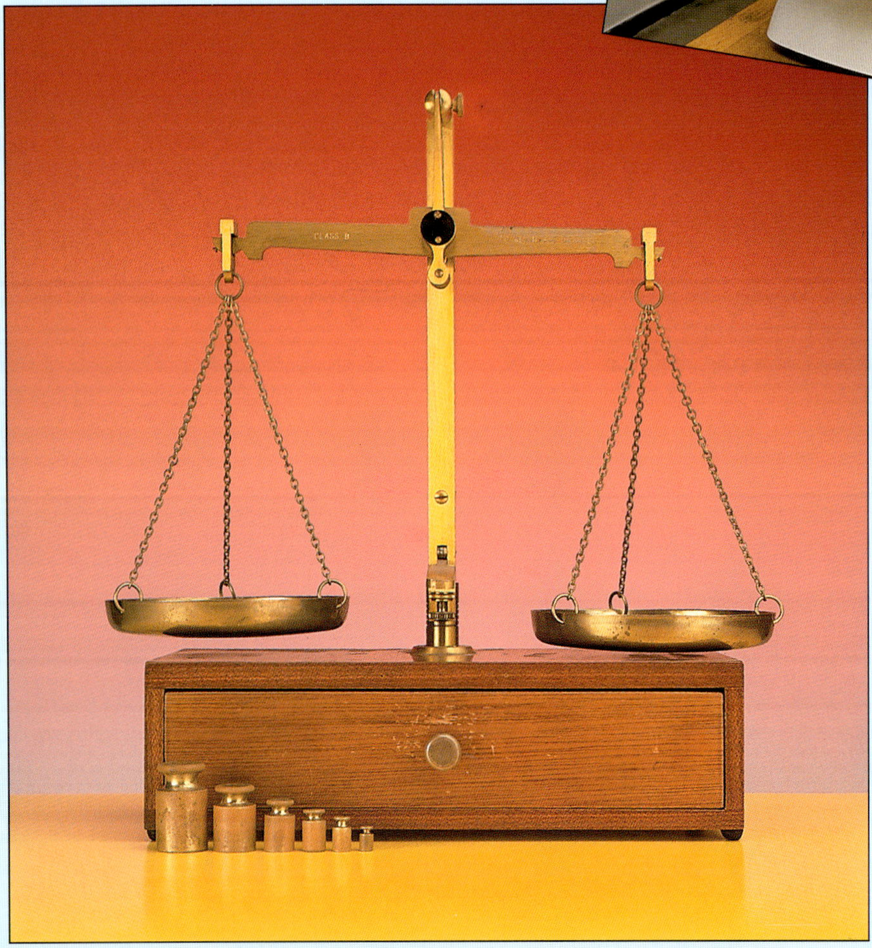

AVERY
Independent
AVERY
1770

WAYMASTER

Sometimes we measure things
by the space they fill...
a cup of flour,
a spoonful of coffee,
a scoop of ice cream,
a handful of sweets,
a bowl of cereal.

But some things are difficult to measure.

We can tell how much water
we have by measuring
the space that it fills.
This jug measures one litre.

A litre of water fills
the same amount of space
as a litre of juice
or a litre of milk.
We use litres to measure volume.
Volume is the space inside
a container.

These containers each hold one litre –
even though each has a different shape.

What can be measured
using these?
Where would you find them?

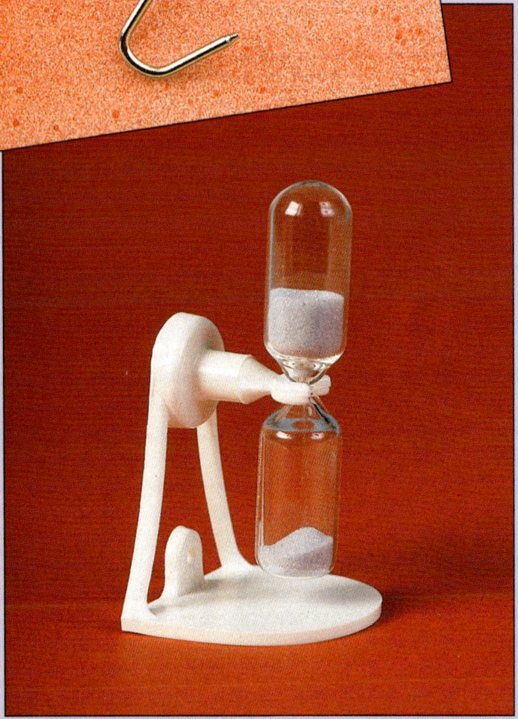

250
200
150
100
50
CENTIMETRES
FLUID OUNCES
10
9
8
7
6
5
4
3
2
1

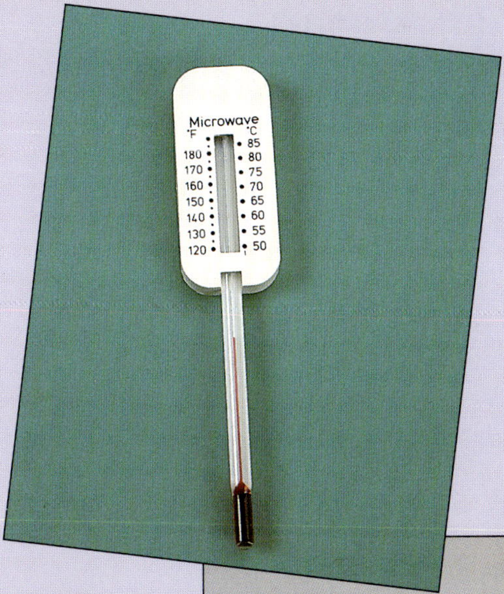
Microwave
°F
°C
180
170
160
150
140
130
120
85
80
75
70
65
60
55
50

1/2 tsp
2.5cc
1 tsp
5cc
1/2 TBS
7.5cc
1 TBS
15cc

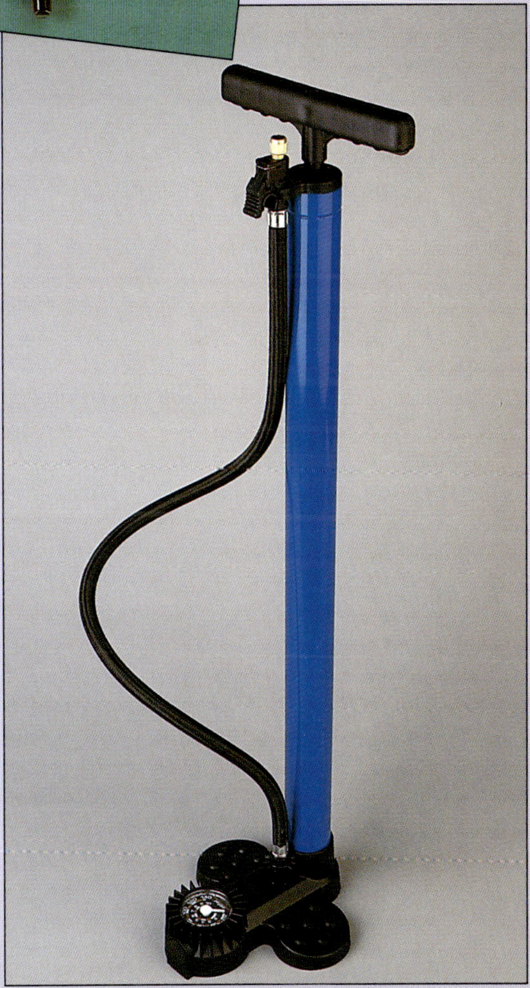

Almost everything can be measured.
How many different ways could you measure these things?

How many things can you measure about yourself?

About this book

All books which are specially prepared for young children are written to meet the interest of the age group at which they are directed. This may mean presenting an idea in a humorous or unconventional way so that ideas which hitherto have been grasped somewhat hazily are given sharper focus. The books in this series aim to bring into focus some of the elements of life and living which we as adults tend to take for granted.

This book develops and explores an idea using simple text and thought-provoking photographs. The words will encourage questioning and discussion – whether they are read by adult or child. Children enjoy having information books read to them just as much as stories and poetry. The younger child may ignore the written words... pictures play an important part in learning, particularly if they encourage talk and visual discrimination.

Young children acquire much information in an incidental, almost random fashion. Indeed, they learn much just by being alive! The adult who uses books like this one needs to be sympathetic and understanding of the young child's intellectual development. It offers a particular way of looking, an approach to questioning which will result in talk, rather than "correct" one word answers.

Henry Pluckrose

BRUTAL SHEFFIELD

Martin Dust

First published in Great Britain in 2021 By Revelations 23 Press

Revelations 23 Press
Unit 11
Neepsend Triangle Business Centre
1 Burton Road
Sheffield
S3 8BW
UK

A CIP catalogue record for this book is available from the British Library.

Softback ISBN 978-1-874171-03-4

Typeset in Clarendon BQ and Helvetica Neue by Martin Dust.

Printed in the United Kingdom

Second Edition

Find Us Here:
www.revelations23.com
www.martindust.photography
www.instagram.com/martindustphotography
www.twitter.com/martindustphoto
www.theblackdogma.com

“I recently spent quite a bit of time in Sheffield, England, which is where I’m from. I wouldn’t move back there, but it’s funny when you spend a bit of time in the place where you were brought up. You kind of realise how that place has had quite a big effect on you or made you a certain way.”

Jarvis Cocker

SYT

Unearthing the Unfinished City

Damon Fairclough

Stashed away in a corner of my house, I've got a small pile of old school exercise books. 'City of Sheffield Education Committee' they say on the front, and each one features my own hesitant scrawl spelling out my name.

I pull the fattest one from the pile and gaze at the cover.

'Geography', it says. 'September 1978'.

I open the book at the first double spread – the first project at the start of a new academic year, in a new school, where I wore scratchy new trousers and a blazer that held me rigid as a plank. Stretching across the two pages is a map – hand-drawn, not to scale. It's a fragment of Sheffield, a tiny portion of the city. But in that September at the back end of the 70s, when I drew it with a nibbled pencil and inked over it in biro, it was roughly nine-tenths of the world I knew.

There's my house and a stubby length of Carterknowle Road. There's an odd scribble to indicate the weird little church we could see from our living room, and then there are the steps and cinder paths and grass banks and woods that lined my ten-minute walk to school. But there the map stops. No hinterland, no environs. Within these few ballpen lines are the doors I knocked on, the gardens I played in, the streets where we went out on bikes.

I flip through a few pages, and there are more maps – some drawn in pencil, like the first, and others in pale pinks, blues and greens. They're the tell-tale pastel shades that reveal these maps had been churned through the school's duplicating machine and handed round by the teacher before being Sellotaped into my book. Little by little, each map expands my world – from the school's wider local area with its Thorntons factory, its quarry, an edge of Millhouses Park, to a map showing the whole of central Sheffield marked with my favourite locations: Redgates toy shop, Western Jean Company, the Gaumont cinema and the Hole in the Road.

I keep turning the pages, keep seeing Sheffield grow as the maps and diagrams proliferate. This one shows rivers, the next one shows motorways, and this one is a slice through the city. 'A Cross-Section of the Don Valley at Tinsley' it says above drawings of steelworks and gasometers, cooling towers and terraced houses. Like a cutaway sketch in a medical text book, it exposes the layers of the city's calloused skin.

The Sheffield in these exercise books is a city of industry, unmistakeably. It's a place where an optimistic future is still being built – just about. It's the city I spent the next few years discovering as I roamed ever further from the first map's truncated childhood kingdom – and it's the place where I learned that the future doesn't always do what it's told.

In 1978, Sheffield was still trying to be the city that post-war planners had hoped it would be: a smoke-free metropolis in which concrete schemes were stacked up and strung out across hillsides, and where a side-burned and mini-skirted population could flit from workplace to leisure palace while grooving to some uptempo jazz-pop. But as I scuttled through its subways, traversed its concrete walkways and took buses that charged fares that cost fuck all, I realised that its benign and beneficent masterplan had gaps in it, and the more you looked, the more you saw an awkward Sheffield that was still poking through.

They'd cleaned up its air, but they hadn't wiped out all its workshops. They'd sliced dual carriageways through its back streets, but in between, they'd left carcasses built from brick. Over here there were arts towers, ziggurats and tower blocks, but over there you'd find factories full of ghosts.

I assumed that in time, Sheffield's new world would be signed off and completed, and such spectral relics would be wiped off its map. Because I was too young to realise that my Sheffield wasn't the last Sheffield – and that a city's future, while often being promised, isn't something that actually arrives.

I get it now, of course. I see it in Martin Dust's mesmerising photographs, in which I see Sheffield's continuing architectural stratification – a process that involves designing tomorrow, and yet never finally drawing the last line. Along the way there have been attempts to wipe out utopias and detonate past certainties, and build new versions of new visions in their place. And yet throughout Martin's photos of the city – images captured between 2018 and 2021 – it seems to me that yesterday is vengeful, and the awkward and stubborn *still* break through.

Now though, it's those nobbled edifices and snarling façades of Sheffield's post-war project that cling on like barnacles to a rock. When I was drawing my maps and discovering my city, these fortress-like housing schemes and arrowhead churches were the architectural shock troops of a future that was still to arrive. But now on page after page, in image after image, they're like the survivors of a battle that's been and gone.

Brutal Sheffield is both a portrait of this environment and an excavation of memory, a trek through the city that provides the context and inspiration for so much of Martin's art. Because while I was walking these streets, peeking round corners, creating Sheffield myths and legends of my own, Martin was mapping his own brutal Sheffield and now these pages reveal something of that tale.

Whether he's uncovering lost rehearsal rooms, remembering ex-record shops, or capturing the poetry of concrete and glass, his photographic world is one in which sullen-faced car parks can conceal fragmented recollections – and become the accidental backdrops to our lives.

I flick back through the pages of my old exercise book and I'm struck by how little of that Sheffield remains. The gasometers and cooling towers, Redgates and the Gaumont, even that great modernist vortex that everyone knew as the Hole in the Road – all erased. And back at the first map I looked at, the story's the same. Every building, except my old house, has now gone.

It's lucky, then, that maps and photographs will still tell their stories. And they'll do it even if that's all we have left.

PANTONE®
Sheffield Grey

Brutal Beauty
Sheffield is full of concrete; it's something you grow to love.

Hobnobs
F
McKee.

Chippy Tea
Things don't have to be complex, find comfort where you can. Rest In Peas.

Modern Life Is Rubbish

In many ways, this is how I think of Sheffield but it isn't, I'm distorting the reality trying to hold onto the past. It's just that it looked more interesting back then. Now we have carbon copies of everything, all on brand.

After visiting Redgates toy shop, I'd visit this shop for a sandwich, usually a Steak Canadian. Years later, I'd switch the visit to Redgates for the arcade around the corner. Sheffield is much duller than I'd have you think. I think we all do this, don't we?

SHEFFIELD
ORGEMAS

Last Practice Of Buzzmuck

Out of nine practice venues I used in Sheffield, this is the last one standing.

Because Sheffield was built off the back of heavy industry there were also thousands of little specialist workshops; they called them Little Mesters.

When the work disappeared, the bands moved in. For £20 a month you'd get a room where you could play and practice all week, then for the rest of the time, you could use it as a bedroom. At that time, catching a taxi back home would cost you two nights out.

We'd shower at the swimming baths, shave at the large department stores early in the morning and just have the best time. It didn't seem to matter that the band was rubbish.

Modern Life Is Rubbish 2

This is Sheffield all over for me. A new building that's been empty for over 10 years, attached to a building that looks like it only just survived World War 2 and to top that off we have a new digital advertising board.

I'll have a bet with you now dear reader, that in 10 years' time it will be exactly the same!

Fresh Cut

O travellers from
somewhere else to here,
Rising from Sheffield Station
and Sheaf Square
To wander through the
labyrinths of air,
Pause now, and let
the sight of this sheer cliff
Become a priming-place
which lifts you off
To speculate
What if..?
What if..?
What if..?
Cloud-shadows drag
their hands across
the white;
Rain prints the sudden
darkness of its weight;
Sun falls and leaves the
bleaching evidence of light.
Your thoughts are like
Set down to decorate

From Sheffield With A Kiss
By chance, another set of homes or student accomodation no-one can afford.

Our Light Is From Mars

Yeah I Know

You're probably thinking of snooker or Ronnie O'Sullivan. I can't blame you, it's funny how just one thing seems to stick as if people can't see any further. The experts might have you believe that we are all getting worse and that we all have ADHD or some other modern condition, but those things weren't available to me growing up.

We are all haunted by our past, trying to escape, trapped inside a Russian doll called Shirley Valentine, trying to get over the past and move on, but like the wood chip wallpaper, it would seem that some things are irremovable.

Sometimes Blue
Not all our skies are grey and I knew as soon as I said it, they wouldn't be.

Go On Then

Sheffield's making is probably its own downfall as well. The fact that you pretty much get left alone up here can be a real benefit but if you're a needy type then it may just not work for you. Sheffield is pretty much a "Go on then, impress me" kind of city and always has been.

I remember playing loads of pubs like the Hallamshire with my punk band and purposely not leaving any gaps between the songs because we didn't want to give the audience a chance to dead air us. I've witnessed The Human League, March Violets and loads of others all get the famous treatment. Let me tell you, it's fucking heartbreaking. Clap, they've probably put a lot of work in.

Sides And Corners

Under The Influencer
What's Your Brand? What's Your Style?
I'm A Photographer, That's It
I Shoot What I Want And Like
Fuck You And Your Content Provider Life
And Then Fuck You Again

On Your Knees
Sheffield must have the largest collection of brutal and modernist churches in the country.

Underpass

The smell of piss, beer and blood from the weekend made these places somewhere to practice your sprint; even when the lights worked, it didn't make them any safer. It must have seemed like a good idea at the time.

The only relief they gave were the latest posters for gigs and releases. Art that you couldn't buy and something you don't see now. I miss that part.

Level 5

Hanging out on the Showboat, wagging school and going to gigs, this is where lessons were learned. Being forced to pay for membership over and over because they knew I was underage. They'd take my money and issue the instruction "Stay away from the bar".

Always leaving with a crowd just in case someone was waiting in the subway or escalator. On to level 5 to pick up my school bag, hidden behind the pipe; it had been there all week.

Virgin, In The Shadow Of

The walk down to Virgin was important. On the way you could take in all the other record shops, endlessly looking at the sleeves and things you just couldn't afford to buy. Even calling in on a couple of sheet music shops to look at the books. The Sex Pistols File was a favourite, I must have read it all over the year it came out but I still don't own a copy! All the hours spent in Virgin checking out the new releases and notices on the wall, it now seems strange to think of how much time we spent hanging out in that shop.

Road To Nowhere
What do you mean you don't have a favourite bridge on the M1?

FUCK THE POLICE

Concrete Curves
Even in the most bleak of locations it still looks like the future.

Two Scoops

When the scooped roof came into sight, it finally meant that you were on your way - seven days in Skegness at the miners' camp. Not only did they work together, but they also holidayed together!

The trip would always start at the Working Men's Club and even the bus journey was an adventure. Egg sandwiches and two cans of pop with all your mates. Then came the brown envelope with your spending money. I remember it being the most money I'd ever received, including birthdays! From memory, I remember this place being a petrol station, Little Chef and now it's a Starbucks.

Reach For The Sky & Just Wait

My first band came into being by a stream in a wooded area close to where I lived. We picked what we wanted to play via a Wilson Peck catalogue of instruments and dreamed about being able to afford and play them. The band name also came from that catalogue as well, The Discontinued, after a guitar they advertised that they no longer made, which was odd. Our older mates already had a punk band and were planning gigs at the local youth club.

Eventually, we'd get enough gear together to make a band and play with our friend's band, the Mau Maus. They were one of the first UK Hardcore bands and we all loved them so much. We played with them a fair bit before they split up and we went on to be another band more in the style of New Model Army.

While it was a great laugh for years, it wasn't really going anywhere. I remember sitting on the Wicker in 1989 outside a cafe and listening to a tape a mate had made of the new craze called House Music. I'd later buy a Roland W30 and never looked back; that one purchase took me around the world a couple of times and still does.

DAIKIN
SkyAir
Active-series
DAIKIN
SkyAir
Active-series

Another Kind Of Chicken Town

I do wonder sometimes if I'm painting a grim picture of Sheffield but the reality for me is that I'd rather capture the buildings I like before they all get turned into grey boxes and student accommodation. I'm not against the students either, some of the best creatives never leave and they also bring a lot of new nights to the town.

What I'm against is Sheffield looking like everywhere fucking else. I can remember the creep of the rundown from the Wicker to Moorfoot. The chicken shops move in and everyone else moves out or shuts down.

You could once have a night out on the Wicker, it had at least 20 pubs. Now it has just three and zero footfall.

I know nothing about town planning but I do know that when the chicken shops move in, the rest of retail moves out, so if you work for the council, make a note.

The fact that we've now become just one or two streets for a night out is a sorry sight but at least all the divs are in one place eh? You'll probably find me in Barry's, at least he still gives me a free pint on my birthday.

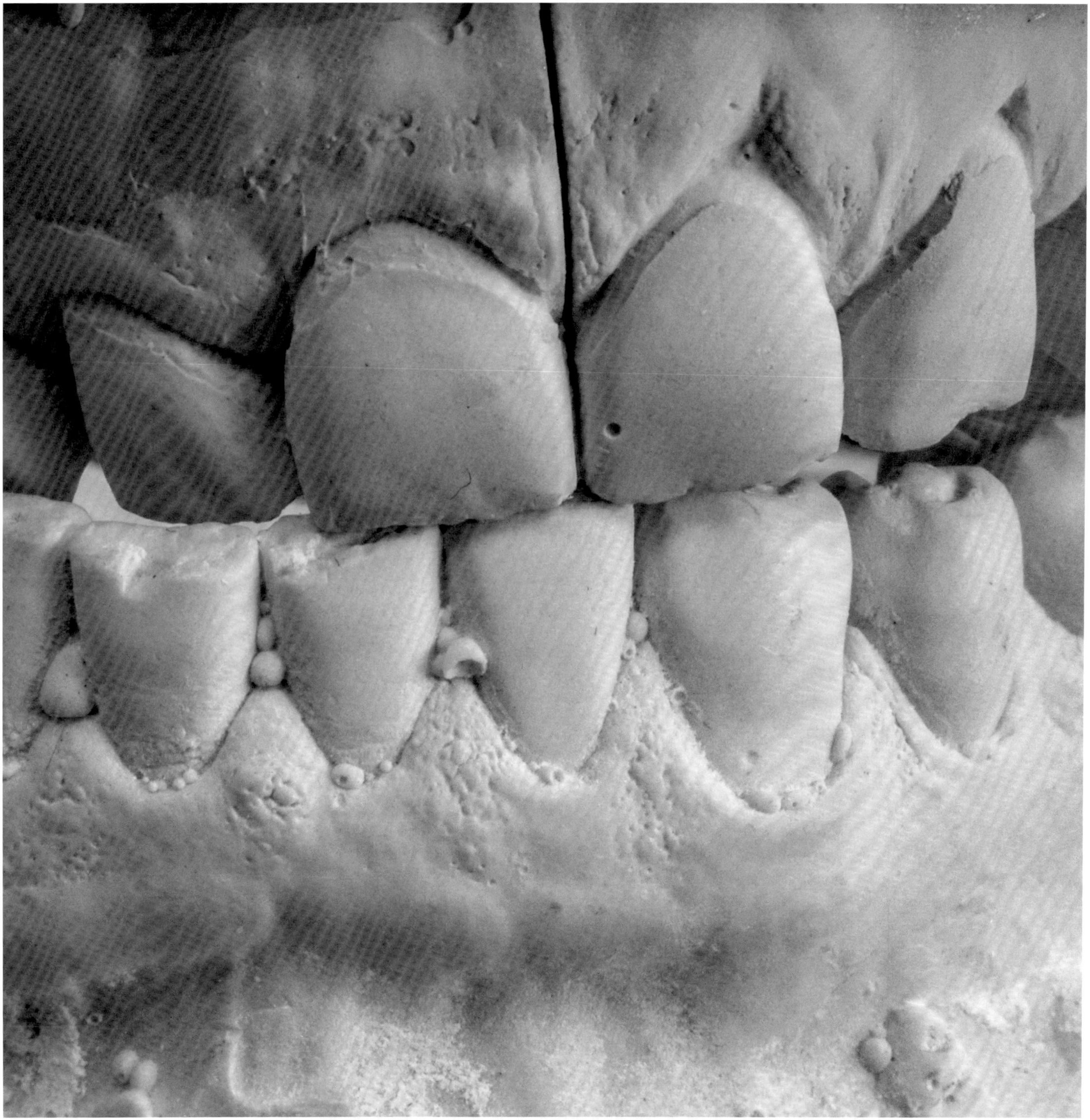

This Place Grinds Your Teeth

Concrete & Steel

For some of us, Concrete and Steel is all we know. Our first house was pre-fabricated and built during the war for the workforces. My grandparents' house was 16 massive slabs of concrete. They are both still standing and being lived in, lasting I predict, well beyond their projected lifetime.

Sheffield had a strange way of incorporating nature but concrete and steel have always overlooked the city and informed it. Work dictated shops and pubs in odd places you'd never expect to see them. They gave a really odd and unique vibe to the city, something I really enjoyed about the place.

A butcher's with a skip outside, full of carcasses; around the corner those dodgy garages you could get your car mended when you couldn't afford a proper place. Up the stairs was a recording studio and loads of practice rooms. Across the internal bridge was a boxing club and on Tuesday night you'd see a very young Prince Naseem doing circuits.

All gone, replaced with steel and uniform buildings that could as easily be in Chicago or Detroit. This isn't about holding onto the past, it's about giving people a place of their own and somewhere they could grow. With house prices as they are, I'd say it's needed now more than ever.

Welcome
NO
UNAUTHORISED
PARKING

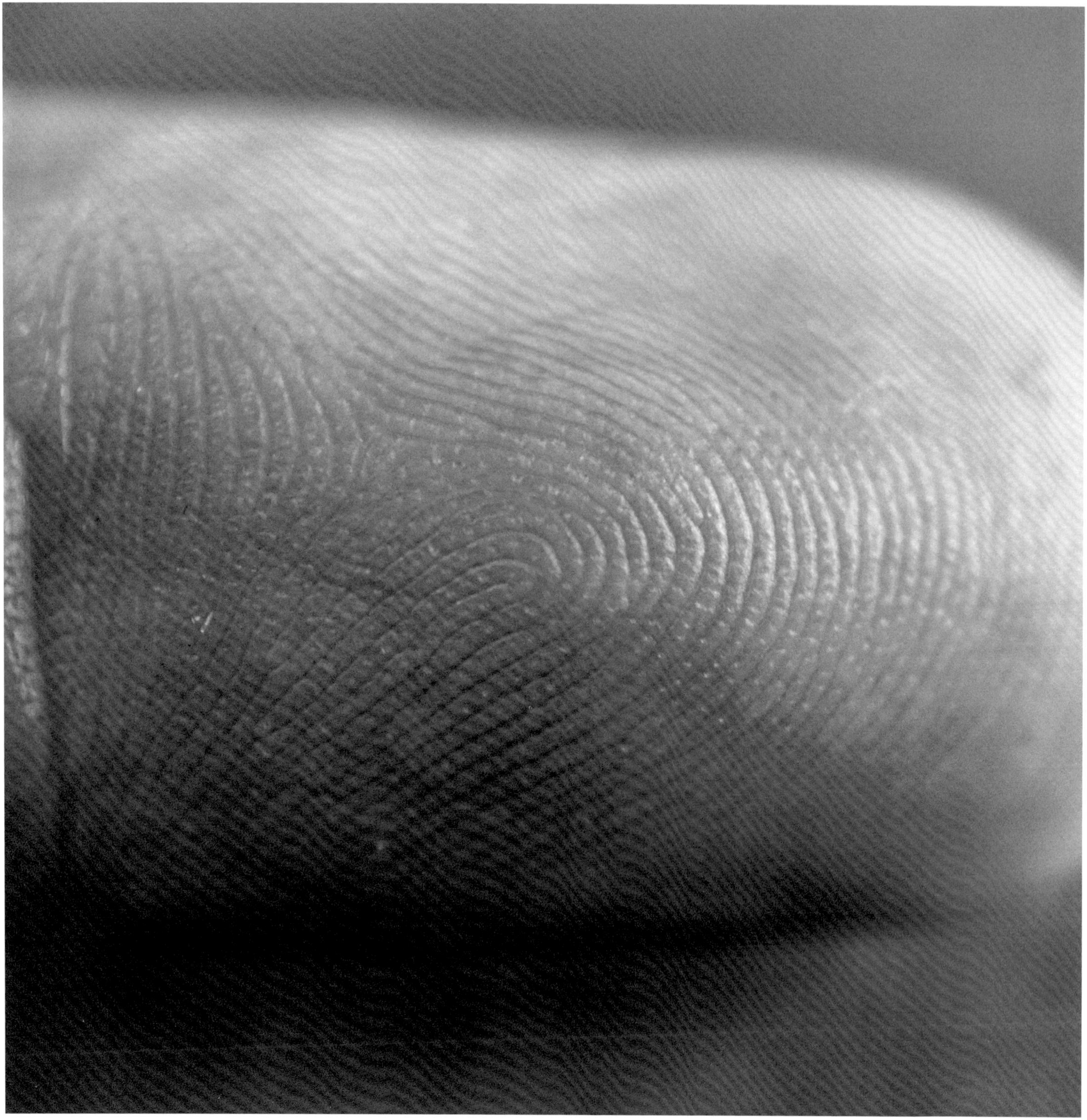

Hoping To Leave At Least A Few Before I Go

South Street

NCP
P

Level 5
The place you'd hide your school bag while nipping to Woolworths for the free 7"s!

KEEP YOUR

Brutal Beauty
Glass, concrete and steel, the materials of choice in SoYo®.

SIGNS
RIME

Good At Being Wrong

If this book has taught me anything then it's persistence. I had to visit some places up to five times just to get the right kind of photograph, whether that's the light, sky or my angle. Often, I'd rush and miss out on the right lines or the exact shot I wanted. Sometimes before a visit, I'd build up a place so much that by the time I got there, I couldn't find anything close to what I remembered. Then you look at the greats like Tish Murtha or Vivian Maier and you can see the answer right there: ordinary is interesting.

When you start out in photography it's hard, trying to find out who you are and what your style or look is. It's caused me to doubt and question everything, even whether I'm good enough. I mean, my opening line is a book. I've questioned that decision many times. Unlike music, photography has made me question even the reality we live in.

My message, if you are starting out, is to just keep going and taking more photographs. Sitting on the sofa won't change anything, learn to be good by being wrong.

Love From Sheffield
Slowly replacing all the Little Mesters one by one, soon there will be nowhere left to practice.

PARKHILL FLATS SHEFFIELD
City Architect: J. L. WOMERSLEY, ESQ., F.R.I.B.A., Dist,TP., M.T.P.I.
Contractors: SHEFFIELD CORPORATION (Public Works Department) Manager Hy. Smith, Esq., A.R.I.C.S
KETTON CEMENT USED
SOLE DISTRIBUTORS
THOS. W. WARD LTD
ALBION WORKS SHEFFIELD

APPLY TOOTH-PRESSURE
AND YOU GET DEAFENING
ACTION; BITE AGAIN AND
THERE'S NOTHING LEFT.
THERE IS A WAY OF
IT'S NOT THE JOB OF ARCHITECTS
TO FORM COMMUNITIES. IT'S THE
JOB OF ARCHITECTS TO MAKE
PLACES WHERE COMMUNITY CAN
HAPPEN IF IT WANTS TO HAPPEN.

D2

YOU

ME DOTH MATE

Sheffield
Hallam
University

The Only Gig

It seems crazy now but at the time of the gig in Park Hill, it was just another event in an unusual venue. I'm not sure why we didn't document it better than we did but I think a large part of my thinking was that it would never happen.

Magazines and event promoters come and go in Sheffield, usually influenced by the new intake of students to the universities. We'd worked with Article Magazine and Drumroll before, and we liked them a lot, so when the event was mentioned, we said we'd help out. When I say help out, I mean give up our fee to ensure we could fly Sandwell District in from Berlin and pay Richard H Kirk to open the night.

Regis from Sandwell said they'd play the event if I got Richard there, got them non-budget flights and tea at the chippy. It sounded like something I could sort. I dropped his agent an email and he came back with a price. I dropped Regis an email to say we couldn't do it and on his advice, I halved the price. His agent went mental for days after but we got the booking. Richard wanted to get there 30 minutes before it started and play as early as he could, all fine by me.

With the line-up sorted we went for a visit with Urban Splash and Human; the place was just a shell and full of dust. More worrying than that was that there was no wall at the end of the building. There was no way we could do a large event with that still open. Urban Splash said they'd sort that out so we didn't have that much to worry about.

The licence for the event was granted and then someone made the mistake of telling the local newspaper, The Star, about the event. While the article was positive, the comments underneath caused us so many problems. As is now the norm, some individuals just sat on the comments section pouring out paranoid hate and bollocks all day long. It wasn't long before the powers above us started to worry about all the shite these individuals were saying and threatened to pull the licence. In the end, to keep the event "secure and everyone happy, we had to pay for a police office to sit outside the event all night. He sat in his car, bored out of his head, and cost us £1500.

Richard turned up in time and immediately regretted saying he wanted to play first. It was 9pm and there was no-one there. The event went really well, a sold-out audience and the room was banging. I wish we'd filmed the event and took more photos but who knew we'd be doing this 10 years later.

drumro[ll], The Black Dog & Article Magazine present...
drumro[ll]
[ll]
1ST BIRTHDAY
PARK HILL, SHEFFIELD
SANDWELL DISTRICT
(SANDWELL DISTRICT)
THE BLACK DOG
(SOMA / DUST SCIENCE)
GEORGE FITZGERALD
(HOTFLUSH / MANMAKEMUSIC)
RICHARD H KIRK
(CABARET VOLTAIRE)
30.09.11
£10/£12/MOTD
Tickets available from:
residentadvisor
SKIDDLE.COM
the uk what's on guide
In association with:
ARTICLE
more info at facebook.com/drumrollclub

RAINDROPS
PILE IN POTHOLES
WITH PRIDE
AS THOUGH
THEY PIERCE
THE CONCRETE
THEMSELVES

ODEON
LUXE

THE ARTS TOWER

Just About Every Night Started Here

Everyone Gets Lonely

Birthday Surprise

Margaret Pearce

Nelson
an International Thomson Publishing company I(T)P®

Melbourne • Albany, NY • Belmont, CA • Bonn • Boston • Cincinnati
Detroit • Johannesburg • London • Madrid • Mexico City • New York
Paris • Singapore • Tokyo • Toronto • Washington

Nelson I T P®
102 Dodds Street
South Melbourne 3205

Email nelsonitp@nelson.com.au
Website http://www.nelsonitp.com

Nelson I T P® ***an International Thomson Publishing company***

First published in 1998
10 9 8 7 6 5 4
05 04 03 02 01 00 99

National Library of Australia
Cataloguing-in-Publication data

Margaret Pearce
Birthday Surprise
ISBN 0 17 009431 6
ISBN 0 17 009414 6 (set).
I. Title. (Series: BlitzIt).
A823.3

Editorial production by BDP
Designed by Christine Deering
Illustrations by Grant Adam/Uncommon Characters
Cover designed by Grant Adam/Uncommon Characters
Text designed by Christine Deering
Typeset in Clearface Regular
Printed in Singapore by Kin Keong Printing Co. Pte. Ltd

A short version of this story appeared in *Reaping a Harvest* by Kavanagh, Kilby and Savage (Longman Cheshire, 1988), and was also published by the NSW Education Department in 1983.

Nelson Australia Pty Limited ACN 058 280 149 (incorporated in Victoria) trading as Nelson ITP.

Contents

Chapter 1

Financial Crisis

Everyone knows what it's like to have the occasional money problem. We had a really bad one. At the time, we had no idea that our lack of money would land us in an out-of-control nightmare from which there seemed to be no escape.

Mum's birthday was only ten days away, so we had to think of something to give her in a hurry. The trouble was, however, that the three of us were broke. We barely had a cent between us. Frazzle, my older sister, was still trying to pay for the window she'd broken in spectacular fashion last month. She'd been trying out her Christmas skateboard on the back porch when the board shot out from under her and right through a window. (Mum and Dad were not pleased. Frazzle'd be paying the bill off for months.) I'd spent my savings on a computer game I'd grown sick of in a week. And Freckles? Our younger sister had a bad case of sweet tooth: any pocket money she had she spent on chocolate, chocolate, and... chocolate.

We'd been discussing Mum's birthday for what seemed like hours, but we still couldn't agree on a present. We had a list of suggestions a page long, but there was nothing on it we could afford.

"A bunch of flowers would be nice; or a flowering plant," Freckles said.

"Who's got any money to buy flowers? Or a plant?" Frazzle asked.

"We could grow some," Freckles replied. She was beginning to look a bit teary. That was always a bad sign.

"In ten days?" Frazzle laughed. "Don't be so stupid."

It looked as if Freckles and Frazzle were heading for a fight. Suddenly, I had a brainwave. The talk of plants got me thinking about something we'd learned at school earlier that week.

"I know what to do! We'll make a hothouse and use the hydroponics method to force the growth of some seeds," I said.

"Do you mind translating that into plain English, Professor?" Frazzle asked, bad-temperedly. She was getting very impatient.

"Okay. This is how we do it..."

• • •

Our science teacher was really enthusiastic about hydroponics. Hydroponics is the technique of growing plants in a mixture of water and fertiliser, instead of soil. It is often used in parts of the world where the soil is poor. It's also used by growers who want to produce plants and flowers in greenhouses for sale to supermarkets and other stores.

It was the second point that got me thinking. Perhaps, if we came up with the right fertiliser mix and a home-made hothouse, we could produce an amazing birthday plant for Mum in super-quick time. At this stage, anything was worth a try! I had no reason to think that the whole thing would go terribly, terribly, wrong . . .

Chapter 2

Hybrid Species

The next morning we set to work in the old shed. The first thing to do was to make the water/fertiliser mix in which the birthday plant would grow.

Frazzle found a couple of dusty old bottles of Mucho-grow plant fertiliser on a shelf, so we poured the contents into an old fish tank that hadn't been used for years. We probably got a bit carried away: also Freckles tossed in some Supa-Gro fish food she'd found, and I added the leftover chemicals from my old chemistry set. To be honest I don't know exactly what they were – the labels had all rubbed off the jars – but the result was a hellish green broth that bubbled and fizzed in the tank.

Frazzle had found an old electric blanket in the spare room. She tucked it carefully around the tank, plugged it into the power point, and turned it on full. I set up my fluorescent desk lamp to shine into the sludgy fertiliser mess covering the bottom of the tank. We had our hothouse; now we were ready for the seeds and plant cuttings.

"I collected some Sweet Pea seeds from old Mrs Smith," Frazzle said. "And a few other cuttings – I don't know what they are, but the plants had enormous flowers." We tossed them into the now steaming mix, and watched them sink into the sludge.

"And I've got something, too," Freckles said. Frazzle and I rolled our eyes, then stared as Freckles produced a tiny cutting. It looked a bit familiar; a fleshy green bud, rather like a tiny head with a creepy, tight-lipped mouth.

"What *is* it?" I asked.

"I nicked a piece of Mr Godfrey's Venus Flytrap," Freckles explained. "He says it's a carnivore. He feeds it meat and flies and stuff, and the plant chomps it all up with its teeth."

"You're disgusting," groaned Frazzle. "Anyway, plants don't have teeth, stupid. You watch too many cartoons."

"I don't think . . ." *we should add it,* I was going to say, but Freckles' bottom lip drooped, so I dropped it in as well. It couldn't hurt . . .

• • •

A day or two later, the Sweet Pea seeds had put up yellow-green shoots, and a lot of tiny roots. The cuttings were sprouting new growth as well.

"Is my plant growing?" Freckles asked, hopefully.

The Venus Flytrap cutting had sent down a

maze of fine hair-like roots, but it didn't appear to have grown.

"It looks very healthy," I assured Freckles.

The days slid past, and the long curling stems of the Sweet Peas and the cuttings grew bigger. Freckles was worried, however. Although the roots of her Venus Flytrap had spread across the tank, almost choking the Sweet Pea roots, the cutting itself wasn't growing.

Every time I turned my back she would pour more and more fertiliser into the tank.

"What are you doing?" I groaned, the first time I caught her.

"I am feeding my plant lots of fertiliser so it will grow big and strong," Freckles explained.

I sighed and left her to it. She looked so pleased, and I didn't want to hurt her feelings. Most importantly, it didn't seem to be harming the plants' growth. With the food, and the warmth, they were thriving. By day seven, the different plants had merged together in the liquid. It was impossible to tell where the Sweet Peas ended and the Venus Flytrap began. The plant – whatever it was now – had long, curling tendrils, covered in buds.

The night before Mum's birthday, the buds opened out. The flowers were like nothing we'd ever seen before – giant purple, pink, blue and red flowers, with a perfume so strong it flooded the shed.

"Mum is going to be so thrilled," Frazzle sighed.

"Except the tank looks dirty and un-birthday present-y," Freckles grumbled.

This was true. Beneath the brightly coloured blossoms, the fish tank was stained and discoloured with green slime, spilt chemicals and lumps of fertiliser powder.

"What if we were to transplant the flowers into Mum's old frypan, and put it on a low heat?" Frazzle suggested. "It won't look as bad, and if we keep the heat on, the plant might grow even bigger."

This was a satisfactory solution. We poured the fertiliser mixture into the frypan, then gently placed the birthday plant into it. After Mum had gone to bed we smuggled it inside and plugged it on the kitchen bench. We felt very pleased with ourselves. Mum would love it!

Chapter 3

Weird Stuff

We were right. It was a very successful birthday present. Mum gasped with pleasure at the brightly coloured, highly perfumed flowers when she came out in the morning.

"You are all very clever to have grown the plant yourselves," Mum said as she gave each of us a kiss and a hug.

"They're Sweet Pea flowers," Freckles said.

"I don't know about that," Mum said with a laugh. "The flowers smell like Sweet Peas, and are the right colours, but they're the wrong shape. The petals are too fat and fleshy."

Suddenly, there was a movement, and Mum backed away from the plant. It was as if a blossom had made a definite *snap* for her nose. Frazzle and I laughed. Mum looked so surprised.

"Goodness!" Mum said. "How very odd!"

"Don't you like it?" Freckles asked, and her bottom lip started to droop.

"It's a lovely birthday present," Mum said. "I'll look after it very carefully." She smiled, then gave the plant another curious look.

• • •

It was then the nightmare really began. At first we didn't know what was happening, of course; only that there were strange things going on in the kitchen. It started when Mum accused our cat of stealing the piece of lamb she had been defrosting for dinner.

"It was just on the bench and, when I turned my back, it vanished! That dratted cat must have taken it!" she complained, chasing Tabby out of the kitchen.

Frazzle and I laughed to ourselves. Our cat *did* have an appetite like an elephant; Mum should have known better that to turn her back on him with food on the bench.

A few days later, a freshly-made chocolate-cream sponge also vanished. Mum had only turned her back for a few seconds.

The three of us denied taking the cake, but Mum was so annoyed she refused to believe us. We were sent to our rooms in disgrace.

"Just confess, you greedy pig!" Frazzle whispered as we stomped off.

"I bet it was you! I saw you checking it out before, when it came out of the oven. You couldn't wait to get your hands on it!" I fired back. We glared at each other in mutual suspicion, while Freckles sulked in silence.

• • •

Later that evening, after Mum and Dad had settled down, we sneaked into the kitchen for a late-night snack. We were eating slices of cheese rolled around raisins, and drinking milk, when I glanced up at the plant. I nudged Frazzle and Freckles, astonished.

The plant's tendrils had unfurled; they were hanging down over the edge of the bench, nearly to the floor. And there was something else...

"It's moving," Frazzle said quietly.

"It opened the cupboard door all by itself," Freckles whispered.

We watched in horrified silence. Two long tendrils snaked into the cupboard, and swung out again, each one twisted around a chocolate biscuit. Then they swung back up towards the blossoms. There was a distinct *snap* as brightly coloured petals closed around the biscuits. When they opened again, the biscuits had disappeared.

"The plant eats chocolate biscuits?" Freckles whispered.

"And steak. I bet it also ate the chocolate cake. What *else* will it eat?" I said, clammy with fear.

Suddenly the door flew open. Mum stood

there, staring at the open refrigerator door and at our cheese slices. She looked cross.

"Back to bed," she ordered.

She stepped into the kitchen, and there was a *crunch* as she trod on a broken chocolate biscuit. She opened the cupboard door. Inside, the biscuit barrel was tipped over and the lid was off. It was completely empty!

"The cake wasn't enough? Now you've eaten all the chocolate biscuits!" Mum said in disgust. "I don't know what's got into you children. Clean your teeth on the way to bed."

I opened my mouth to protest, then shut it again. There was no way Mum would believe that the plant had eaten the chocolate-cream sponge as well as all the chocolate biscuits. If we hadn't seen the plant eat the biscuits with our own eyes, we wouldn't have believed it either!

It wasn't a joke any more. Tomorrow, I would trash the hungry, thieving plant!

Chapter 4

The Plant Must Go!

“James!” Mum said. “What are you doing?”

It was Saturday morning, and Mum and Dad had gone off to do the shopping. They’d come back earlier than I expected!

I was at the back door, holding the frypan. In the morning light the plant looked more innocent than ever. The flowers were thick and bright. The thieving tendrils were tucked under the blossoms. Mum might have been fooled, but I wasn’t.

"I was taking the plant out to water it," I said, trying to look innocent. Actually, I was taking it to the incinerator to burn it.

"Leave it alone," Mum said. She snatched the frypan off me, put it down on the bench, and re-plugged it into the power point. "It's doing so beautifully. It grows bigger every day."

"Yeah," I said, and went outside.

"I hate you," Freckles said when she saw me. She was on the swing, crying. "You're a nasty, greedy, Jim-pig."

"Me?! What've I done?"

"You snitched all my lollies. I would've shared them."

"You didn't leave them on the kitchen bench, did you?" I asked.

Freckles stopped crying; she looked worried. I hastily groped for my last dollar coin.

"Go and buy some more lollies," I said. "If I took them, I didn't mean to and I'm sorry."

Freckles took my dollar, smiled and skipped

off to the shop. That plant had to go. The thieving was getting past a joke.

• • •

The day got worse. Dad made an apple pie and it vanished. He accused us of stealing it. That evening, the remains of the roast vanished off the carving plate in between us clearing the table and doing the dishes.

Mum and Dad were furious! Mum called Tabby a thief, and ordered him to be fed and kept outside.

"But the stray will eat his dinner," Freckles protested.

The stray was a scruffy-looking Persian. The family that had owned it had shifted four months ago. By rights, the cat should have been taken to the animal shelter, but it was a bit wild and no-one could catch it.

"Too bad," Mum snapped. "I think Tabby's had more than enough to eat for one day."

None of us were game to tell Mum what

had really happened. Poor Tabby was put outside to fight the stray for his food. And I started racking my brains again. Present, or no present...the plant had to die!

Chapter 5

The Plant Strikes Back

The next morning, as the sun was rising, I sneaked into the kitchen. I'd been awake almost all night, planning this. When I *had* drifted off to sleep I'd been woken by what sounded like a dog yelping. Or perhaps it was a nightmare...

Anyway, I had it all worked out. All I had to do was to tip the plant into the incinerator, pour kerosene over it, and light it. The plant would be ashes before anyone else was awake!

I noticed that the back door had been left open overnight. Dad always got uptight if the house was left unlocked so I pushed it shut, and turned my attention to the frypan.

In the matter of a few hours, the plant had grown and grown. The frypan cord and the power point were draped with masses of green tendrils – and the tendrils were covered in spikes! I grabbed a pair of kitchen tongs and whipped the cord from the power point.

I jumped back as the tendrils uncurled from the cord and lashed spikily towards me. They were incredibly long; whip-like and stringy and covered with fine green hairs. They snaked all the way across the room after me until I shut the door on them.

I snuck back to my bedroom to prepare myself for a battle. I pulled my baseball mask from a cupboard, and dressed myself in the thickest clothing and all the protective gear I could find.

Wearing my armour, I opened the kitchen door cautiously. The hairs on the back of my neck lifted in shock and fear. The plug of the frypan was back in the power point. Did this mean the plant was intelligent; that it had a *brain*?

All its tendrils were retracted, tucked up under the fleshy flowers. Once again it looked like a normal flowering plant. However, the flower heads turned towards me as I came closer.

The tendrils unwound as I reached to pick up the frypan. Despite the padded gloves, the heavy overcoat, the scarf and the mask I wore, I cringed, expecting an attack.

Suddenly there were a succession of thundering crashes. The tendrils had wrapped around Mum's prized willow pattern canisters, and flung them to the floor. The china had smashed into a million pieces!

There was a shout, and the kitchen door

swung open. Dad stood there in his pyjamas, clutching a baseball bat. Mum peered over his shoulder.

"James! What *are* you doing!" Dad yelled as he spotted me, and the mess on the floor.

"Just getting breakfast," I apologised.

"In that weird get-up?"

"I was cold."

"You scared the life out of me. I thought we had burglars," he said.

"You can pay for the canisters out of your pocket money," Mum said. "Now, clean that mess up."

I glared at the plant. Once again its tendrils were tucked up neatly out of sight. Mum stood over me and watched until everything was cleaned up.

Chapter 6

A Taste of Blood

Later that day, I sprawled on the back lawn with Frazzle, and whispered to her about what had happened. Dad was around the front mowing the lawn; Mum was poking around the vegie patch. Freckles came skipping out from the house holding a banana.

"Close that kitchen door properly," Mum called. "That thieving stray will get in."

The stray hadn't moved from our place since Tabby's food bowl had been put outside.

Freckles turned to shut the door but it was too late. The stray had shot inside.

"Get that animal out of my house," Mum ordered. "Now!"

Frazzle and I scrambled to our feet and ran towards the kitchen. Suddenly, the stray let out a blood-curdling screech. However, when we got inside, it was nowhere to be seen. In the kitchen there was a strange, decaying, meaty, smell – as if something was going off.

One of the large blossoms of the plant was closed like a large, un-wholesome bud, the tentacles still retracting. Frazzle nudged me and pointed. I stared at the plant more closely. The large bud suddenly quivered as if something was struggling inside it. Then the quivering stopped, and there was a sound like a *gulp*. The bright pink colour of the bud deepened to dark red.

Frazzle looked at me. Her face was white and scared.

"I don't believe it," I said, but I did! I had to believe it! The plant had snatched up and eaten the stray!

After we got over the shock, we told Mum that we had sent the stray away. Then we went for a walk to have a council-of-war.

"Do you reckon it's possible the plant is a sort-of hybrid Venus Flytrap and Sweet Pea plant?" Frazzle whispered.

I shrugged. We kept walking. We passed the Timbols' place. Their gates were open, but their miniature terriers didn't come out and yap at us as we passed, as they usually did. Mr Timbol gave us a grumpy nod.

"Where are your dogs, Mr Timbol?" Frazzle asked.

"They're hiding under the house. They strayed off somewhere last night, then came yelping back home as fast as their little legs could carry them. It's as if they're terrified of something, or someone," Mr Timbol grumbled.

"You kids didn't scare them last night, did you?" He glared at us suspiciously as we said "No".

"What if they snuck in the kitchen door last night?" Frazzle whispered as we walked off. "Didn't you say it was open?"

There was a lot to think about. Suppose the plant unlocked and opened the back door? Suppose it gave off a smell that attracted animals? Then I had a terrible thought. "So the blossoms are carnivorous! What if they get big enough to eat... *a human*!?"

Frazzle and I looked at each other in horror, and ran back home. All I could think of was Mum and Dad and Freckles, pottering around in the kitchen. What if we were too late?!

Chapter 7

Die, Plant, Die!

We both went flying into the kitchen. Everything looked normal. Mum was peeling spuds, Dad was making bread, and Freckles sat at the table eating out of a cake basin.

The kitchen was filled with the overpowering perfume of the blossoms. The decaying meaty smell that had stunk out the kitchen earlier was completely gone. Mum looked away, and a tendril slid out and scooped up a peeled potato.

"What can I do for you two?" she asked.

"Dinner will be ready in about an hour."

"We were thinking that now that your birthday is over, and the plant is starting to die, perhaps we should throw it out," Frazzle said, looking at me for support.

"Throw out my lovely plant?" Mum looked at Frazzle curiously. "It's lovely and healthy, and growing magnificently."

The blossoms wafted more perfume in her direction, and a tendril sneaked another potato and an onion while her back was turned.

"We have to do something," Frazzle whispered as we went outside again. "What if it attacks Freckles?"

"I'll do something," I gritted. "Trust me."

After we finished the dishes and cleaned up that night, I studied the plant. The big fleshy blossoms crowded out of the frypan, a striking mixture of pinks, blues, purples and reds. All the tendrils were neatly looped up under the flowers.

I waited until the house had settled down

for the night. "Going to bed right now," I called, but first I zipped into the kitchen and turned the frypan on high. The tendrils stirred, but I was already out of the kitchen and shutting the door.

In the morning, when we came down to breakfast, all of the blossoms were bright red – but the plant looked healthier than ever!

"Some idiot turned up the control on the frypan," Mum grumbled. "It might have damaged the plant if I hadn't noticed it this morning."

• • •

After that, we waited for Freckles after school every night, and walked home with her. We didn't want to let her out of our sight. I kept having nightmares about her and Mum being in the kitchen without us around. Mum worked part-time, but she was usually home before us.

The next night I sneaked out and tipped a large tin of paint stripper over the blossoms and tendrils. It cost me my week's pocket money to buy – luckily Mum had forgotten about the canisters. The plant cringed back as I poured the paint stripper over it, and made no effort to attack me. I'd done it – at last!

The next morning, however, all of the blossoms were bright blue, and the plant looked healthier than ever. Frazzle gave me a despairing look as we finished our breakfast and escorted Freckles to school.

Mum was in a bad mood before dinner that night. A T-bone steak, ten sausages and half a fruitcake had vanished.

"What are you kids up to?" she stormed. "I just turn my back for a second and you pinch the fruitcake. And someone left the back door open to let the cat steal the steak!"

We denied taking the cake, or knowing anything about the meat. I gave the plant a filthy stare and it fluttered its petals back at me. It seemed to know that it didn't have to hide its appetite from us, only from Mum.

As soon as she left the room those thieving tendrils curled around the kitchen, carrying oranges, apples and bananas to the blossoms, which crunched through the fruit noisily.

In the centre of the blossoms were what I had assumed were circles of yellow stamens. Now they were bigger, and I could see that they were actually razor sharp. Once the petals folded over into their bud shape, I could almost see the food being gulped down the stem.

• • •

The next night I poured weed-killer into the frypan, and the night after that I used up all the fly-spray. We didn't have any caustic soda at home, so I pinched some from the science laboratory at school, and added that too. Every morning, though, no matter what I did to it, the plant looked healthier than it had the day before. It seemed to *thrive* on toxic chemicals! It had even stopped attacking me when I came in to pour poisonous stuff on it. The blossoms actually lifted their heads as if they were enjoying what I was feeding them.

The blossoms were getting larger, and nearly covered half the bench. They certainly weren't pretty any more with their big, fleshy, red, purple and blue petals, but Mum kept going on and on about how beautiful and decorative her birthday plant was. That plant, and its dreadful appetite, looked like being with us... forever!

Chapter 8

People Eater!

On Thursday, Dad was due home late – he had a school reunion, or something. That night we were all woken up by Dad pounding down the passage, calling out to Mum. I squinted a look at the time. It was three o'clock.

Something was going on! I shuffled out of bed and poked my head out the door. Opposite me, Frazzle's door opened as well. Dad rushed back down the passage to the kitchen. He looked a bit shocked.

"What'samatter, Dad?" I asked.

"Shut those doors and stay in your bedrooms," he snapped to me and Frazzle. "There's someone lying on the kitchen floor."

Frazzle and I looked at each other and shut our doors. I sat on my bed and waited. I heard Mum's urgent voice as she phoned someone. Shortly after that the wail of a police siren came closer and stopped. There was the sound of car doors slamming, and the sound of more cars pulling up.

There was the murmur of voices in the kitchen. I heard Dad shush Mum a few times. After a while the back door creaked as it opened. People must have left. Car doors slammed and several cars drove away. Everything was quiet again.

Dad and Mum trudged up the passage together. I sneaked my door open. "What was that all about, Mum; Dad?"

"I've told you all about leaving that back

door unlocked," Dad muttered. "A burglar broke in."

"Anything stolen?" Frazzle asked.

"No. He must have slipped on the floor, and knocked himself out," Mum said. "I think I should stop polishing the lino."

"Are you sure?" I asked. Frazzle and I looked at each other meaningfully.

"The police still have to find out exactly what happened," Dad said. "He came to after a few minutes, and started screaming and moaning something about a killer plant. Must have been raving drunk or off his head on drugs or something. And when the police tried to take him out to the car, there was a plant tendril wrapped so tightly around his ankles it was almost cutting off the circulation. What he was doing with Mum's plant, I have no idea. Now, back to bed. It's a school day tomorrow."

Frazzle looked across the passage at me. Her eyes were wide with terror. I felt myself shaking as I stared back at her. I knew exactly what she was thinking!

The plant was now big enough, vicious enough and hungry enough to attack an adult!

Chapter 9

Until Death Us Do Part

For a while there was a mystery about what had happened to our burglar. Apart from a cut on his head from the side of the bench, and his terror of a "killer plant", there were no other injuries.

"The poor old fellow was always being hauled in for petty thieving," the policewoman explained. "I don't know exactly what happened in there, but it might be enough to stop him for a while!"

We all nodded in agreement. I sneaked a look at the plant. To me, it had a smug, self-satisfied look about it. I didn't believe the back door had been left unlocked. I suspected the plant had enticed the burglar in, then tried to scare him to death.

The plant's blossoms were now the size of large sunflowers, and crowded out most of the bench space. Mum was talking of getting Dad to build a special stand for it in the kitchen.

"It's such an amazing plant," she said. "I really enjoy having it around."

"It's got an appetite like a horse," said Frazzle bitterly one night, as we watched the tendrils open the refrigerator.

One tendril scooped up an opened tin of cat meat, and another tendril curled around the ham slices Mum had bought for our lunch.

"And a digestive system like a goat," I snarled, watching the cat food – tin and all – vanish into a purple blossom. There was a meaty burp as it started on the ham.

"It's not its fault," said Freckles, defensively. "The poor thing is always hungry." She handed half her honey sandwich to a questing tendril. "I think it's cute."

"What about the burglar?" Frazzle asked. "That wasn't very cute."

Freckles just shrugged. "The plant was only protecting us from harm. We need a watchdog around the place now that Philby has wandered off."

I winced. I had my own suspicions about what happened to our dog, Philby, but I wasn't going to upset Freckles by mentioning it. Then again, maybe he'd just run away.

"We have to do something," Frazzle said as Freckles left the room.

"Mum won't hear of us getting rid of the plant," I grumbled. "And nothing I try works. It only seems to make the plant stronger."

"The worst thing is that Freckles, like Mum,

absolutely loves it," Frazzle said with a sigh. "She's always collecting leftovers from my school cooking class for it."

"And it's getting bigger and bigger and more dangerous than ever," I snarled. "We're going to be stuck with it until death us do part."

"Whose death?" Frazzle whispered.

"It had better not be ours," I warned through gritted teeth.

The plant must have understood me. It licked its petals and hosed a wave of strong perfume at me.

Chapter 10

At Last!

The next night, I tried a different sort of extra-strong weed-killer on the plant, but my heart wasn't in it. I had used up all my pocket money for weeks, buying different plant and animal poisons, but the plant seemed to *enjoy* them.

However, one Saturday morning we were woken by the sound of Mum crying out in the kitchen. My first thought was of the plant. It had attacked Mum! I hurtled into the kitchen, my heart in my mouth, with Frazzle close behind me.

Mum stood in the centre of the kitchen, unharmed. Tears were rolling down her cheeks.

"My beautiful birthday plant has died," she sniffed.

There was an overpowering stench of decay in the kitchen. All the brightly coloured, fleshy blossoms had wilted and turned a dirty brown. The tendrils and leaves were dried-up and shrunken. I couldn't believe it! The killer plant was dead at last! What had been powerful enough to kill it when all the poisons I had used had been so useless?

"Sweet Peas usually die after they finish flowering," I stuttered.

"I know," Mum said, holding her nose. She sounded quite upset. "But it was such a beautiful plant. Throw it out, then."

I emptied the plant, with its wilted brown flowers, leaves, tendrils and the thick, decaying sludge of roots, into the incinerator. I saturated the mess with kerosene and lit it. I wasn't taking any chances.

Despite the wet, sloppy, roots, it burned furiously. I think all the petrol and weed-killer saturating the roots must have helped.

As the thick, oily, smoke rose up into the still morning air, Frazzle scrubbed and scrubbed at the frypan with bleach and disinfectant until it was spotlessly clean.

"No need to take any chances," she muttered.

Freckles came to watch us. She was very mournful, and her face was still tear-stained.

"My beautiful plant," she said. "And I gave it such a lovely feed last night."

Frazzle and I came to attention. Had our little sister unknowingly fed the plant the one thing it couldn't eat?

"What did you feed it?" I asked.

"The scones thrown out of Frazzle's cooking class. Miss Redlar said I could have them for our chooks when I asked."

"Our scones were a big disaster," Frazzle remembered. "Thirty kids in the class and fifteen trays of scones. Only one scone got eaten, then Amanda Wallace had to go to sick-bay."

"The poor plant is alway so hungry that I thought I would give it a really decent feed. I piled the scones high on the bench last night. Every one of them was gone by morning," Freckles sniffled. "It must have taken the plant all night to eat them."

I started to laugh. I cackled and cackled. I couldn't stop. I didn't know whether I was hysterical with relief because the ominous threat lurking in our kitchen was gone at last, or because my funny bone was working overtime.

"What's so funny?" Frazzle demanded.

"The plant died of indigestion," I stammered. "All those scones. The Year Five cooking class is a pack of Lucrezia Borgias."

"Who's Lucrezia Borgias?" Freckles asked.

I couldn't answer. I was too busy dodging

Frazzle as she chased me around the yard swiping at me with the frypan.

Frazzle never did have a sense of humour about the messes she and her friends produced in their cooking classes!

About the Author

Margaret Pearce started her career as a copywriter in an advertising agency, and took seriously to writing fiction during the chaotic years of raising children. She is a compulsive reader of books of all types, and a compulsive writer. Margaret lives and works in an underground house in the hills near Melbourne.

BlitzIt

Hell-ectric Guitar

by Brian McGinn

Frank meets a mysterious old man who sells him a battered guitar. The guitar can make him a superstar – but what does it, and the old man, want in return? Will Frank last long enough to enjoy his fame?

Expiry Date

by Raewyn Caisley

Quentin and Andrew think it's pretty funny to tease Richard Corelli. Things go terribly wrong however, and Andrew finds himself haunted by a mysterious stranger. Could Andrew be approaching his "expiry date"?

Blitz It

The Twins in the Trunk

by Susan Green

When Katie finds an old trunk in the cellar under her house, she thinks she's found bushranger's treasure. What she has found is ghost trouble – and double trouble at that!

Katie and Angus soon find that some things are better left unopened...

Monopillar

by Alan Horsfield

A weird alien mystery set in and around Sydney's Powerhouse Museum. Who are the mysterious scientists, and why are they carrying bags of bones around? And why is the Monorail looking so strange?

BlitzIt

BlitzIt **is here! Once you've read one** ***BlitzIt*** **book, you'll want to read them all.**

Mystery ... adventure ... alien visitors ... weird science ... spooky happenings ... ***BlitzIt*** **has something for everyone!**

Bargains from Outer Space

by Heather Hammonds

Rod and Sean get more than they bargain for when they flick through the channels on the new TV. Who, or what, are the strange creatures selling fantastic gadgets? And do they really deliver? Find out what happens when Rod and Sean go on a shopping spree that is out-of-this-world!